Baby Farm Animals

Baby Horses

By Nick Rebman

level
1
little blue
readers

www.littlebluehousebooks.com

Little Blue House is distributed by North Star Editions:
sales@northstareditions.com | 888-417-0195

Produced for Little Blue House by Red Line Editorial.

Photographs ©: Shutterstock Images, cover, 4, 7, 9, 11, 12, 15, 16–17, 18, 21, 23 (top), 23 (bottom), 24 (top left), 24 (top right), 24 (bottom left), 24 (bottom right)

Library of Congress Control Number: 2021916724

ISBN
978-1-64619-476-6 (hardcover)
978-1-64619-503-9 (paperback)
978-1-64619-556-5 (ebook pdf)
978-1-64619-530-5 (hosted ebook)

Printed in the United States of America
Mankato, MN
012022

About the Author

Nick Rebman is a writer and editor who lives in Minnesota. He enjoys reading, drawing, and taking long walks with his dog.

Table of Contents

Baby Horses

A baby horse is born.

It is wet at first.

The baby horse tries to stand up.

Soon it can walk.

The baby horse has
big ears.
It has long legs.

ear

leg

Now the baby horse
can run.

It runs in a field.

field

Eating and Drinking

At first, the baby horse stays near its mother.

It drinks her milk.

Soon the baby horse stops drinking milk.
It starts eating grass.

grass

The baby horse also

needs water.

It drinks from a trough.

trough

Play and Sleep

The baby horse likes to play.

It runs and jumps.

The baby horse sleeps a lot.

It takes many naps.

The baby horse stays outside on warm days. It goes inside a barn on cold days.

Glossary

barn

legs

field

trough

Index